Searching For Peace

Asha Godhia

BookLeaf Publishing

India | USA | UK

Dedication

To my readers, may you find the courage, joy, and love
contained within these pages.
Thank you for your support and belief in me and my
writing.

Whoever you are, no matter how lonely, the world offers
itself to your imagination, calls to you like the wild
geese, harsh and exciting—over and over announcing
your place in the family of things."
Mary Oliver

Preface

Hope whispered softly in my ear,
Inviting me to release my thoughts,
To set them free.

This collection of poems emerges from an exploration of love and loss, hope and despair. Each piece captures those messy emotions we all feel while searching for a bit of peace in this crazy world.

Thank you for joining in this exploration of the heart.

Acknowledgements

Thank you to my family and friends who have stuck by me, have checked in on me, and supported me. You make this journey through life so much richer.

To the readers—thank you for taking the time to engage with these poems. Your willingness to connect with my words means everything. This collection is as much yours as it is mine.

Tethers

I look towards the open door,
I hear the birds calling out
I can feel the warmth of the sun on my skin.

I make my way towards the door,
And just as it is within reach,
I am pulled back
Unable to move forward.
To step over the threshold.

I am rooted
I am stuck
Frozen.

How do I break free
Of the bindings holding me in place?
The insecurities
The fear
The inability to make a decision
To take the next step.

I stand, willing myself to move
Over the threshold
Through the door and
Out into the light.

Invisible chains weigh me down
Holding me back
Denying me what it is I want the most

To leave
To be free
To breathe.

To release the self-doubt
To release the pressure that
Causes paralysis.

I close my eyes
And take a deep breath.
A flicker of light
Through the smallest of cracks
Offers the slightest glimmer of hope.

I open my eyes and look down at my feet.
I lift up my foot
Ready to take that first step.

Feelings

So many thoughts,
So many feelings,
So difficult to articulate.
To put into coherent thoughts,
Into words that make sense.

I'm afraid if I start,
The words won't stop.
Feelings of
Anger
Frustration
Hurt
Distrust
Hatred
Will it ever end?

How long to wait
Before I can feel
Love
Compassion

Understanding
Tolerance
Peace

My heart waits
My breath stills
And I close my eyes.

Sunday Morning

From the sanctuary that is my bed
I open my eyes and take in my surroundings
From the clothes on the floor
To the books on the dresser,
The cup of tea sitting on my nightstand
Reminding me of the movie we watched last night.
I feel a shift in bed and I turn over
You open your eyes and lean over for a kiss
I willingly oblige as our arms wrap around each other
Our bodies move closer until
Our legs are intertwined.
My heart starts to race
As we embrace
We pull up the covers and let our feelings take over.

Road Trip

The continuous road stretches into
Long windy streams of black
The expansive blue sky stretching as far as I can see
Wispy clouds scattered
Creating collages of shapes
Fit for a child's imagination with limitless possibilities

As we pass over hills and deep into valleys
The change in landscape is evident
From the vegetation to the temperature
Warming with each passing minute

The further south we drive
The lighter I feel
The weight of responsibility
Dropping away as the trees get taller
And the grass becomes greener

With each passing mile
The freer I feel
As we get closer to our destination
The ocean teases us with its presence

The waves call out to us
Inviting us in
Excited for our visit
Hoping that we're planning on staying awhile.

Rose Coloured Glasses

The view from rose coloured glasses
Shattered
Replaced with a clear lens
Broken
Distorted
Thrown to the ground
Fractured

Do you see us now?
In all our glory
With nothing to hide
Nowhere to go

Drifting, searching
Looking for a place to land
A place to belong

The world can't save you
Behind those rose-coloured glasses

Now lying there
Broken
Shattered
Casting fractured shadows on the wall

Reflections from the sun
From deep within our memories
Belonging to a different time
A different place

But now
Forced to be here
In the present,
No filters
Wishing for the view from
Rose-coloured glasses

The Day Things Changed

I felt a shift long before it happened
The distance growing, widening
Creating a deep and bottomless chasm

The space between us expands, forming a vast divide
Immeasurable silence
Heavy and oppressive
Settles over us like a shroud
Going on for stretches at a time

Being in the same room
Yet being so far apart
Seconds turning into minutes, into hours
Words unspoken
Thoughts and conversations left unsaid
Never to be shared

A heaviness hangs in the air
Like a thick fog
Dense and unyielding

Light, unable to break through
Searches for a way out
Wanting to pass through
But is forced to accept
The undeniable truth

Light lingers,
Suspended in the dense fog,
And so do I,
Curious to see what happens next

A Peaceful Sanctuary

Nestled in the embrace
Of a cloud-like, oversized comforter
I burrow further into its depths
Drawing the soft folds
Over my shoulders
Along my neck
Tucking them under my chin
I cocoon myself tighter still
Shutting out the harsh light
The constant noise
And the relentless thoughts
That spiral endlessly in my mind
A perpetual whirlwind
Of internal dialogues
Leading nowhere
Offering no peace
I let my eyelids fall
And surrender to the descent

Anger

Hot, fiery anger
Coursing through my veins
Ready to set alight
To anything in its path

Scorching, blinding agony
Obscures my vision
Clouds my thoughts
Shatters comprehension

Bolts of lighting
Thunderous roars
Breaking free from their chains
Ready to demolish anything in its path

A ray threatens to break through
Forcing its way through the dark stormy clouds
A small glimmer dares to seep in

Breaking up the anger
Dissolving the tension
Gradually creating space

Drawing in a sense of calm
I shut my eyes
And squeeze them tight

My breath slows
My heartbeat steadies
I open my eyes
And embrace the light

Unrest

Thunder cracks through the silence
Its rumble echoing through the air
I sit in my room, watching the rain
Zigzagging down my window

A thought forms in my mind
Unexpected, sudden
I pause
Letting it roll over in my mind

Where did it come from?
Why now?
Should I hold onto it? Reflect on it?
Or should I release it back into the abyss?

Like the raindrops on the glass
Vanishing as they slide further down
Falling to unseen depths below
This thought could vanish too

I sit, caught in the space
Between reflection and release
As the raging storm outside
Mirrors the unrest within

Shattered

A million fragments lie shattered at my feet,
Pieces of my heart,
Like broken glass,
Casting splintered reflections on the wall of lost
possibilities.
I reach down to gather the shards,
Cautious not to cut myself
On the memories,
The dreams of what might have been.
Shattered and heartbroken,
Where do I start?
How do I begin
To mend these pieces
And rebuild myself anew?

The Night Sky

The crunch of gravel breaks the silence of the night,
As we carefully make our way closer to the water's edge,
Our steps measured and deliberate,
Guided only by the beam of a flashlight.
As we approach our destination,
We turn off the light and are instantly enveloped in
darkness.
Our breath catches as we look up,
Our eyes slowly adjusting to the night.
Countless stars begin to reveal themselves,
Twinkling and shining,
Millions of tiny specks lighting up the sky.
A shooting star streaks across the heavens,
Gone in the blink of an eye.
I smile,
Filled with gratitude,
Thankful for this moment,
For the beauty that surrounds us in the stillness of night.

A Moment of Gratitude

The sounds of the waves
Crashing against the rocks
A bird calls out over the water
Rooted in place, I draw a deep breath,
Attempting to quiet my thoughts
Willing myself to be in the moment

I spy the sun peaking over the horizon
I open my heart and my mind
The sun rises higher
Bathing the world in golden warmth
I bask in its glory
Feeling its energy course through me
Offering its life force to the earth

The healing energy
Filling me with a sense of tranquility
I breath deeper

Humbled to be in its presence
Grateful to be in this moment
Thankful to be alive.

Knots of the Past

A heaviness settles in my heart,
Making its presence known like a burden.
Old wounds, tangled thoughts, actions—
All mixed together,
A chaotic mess
Like a knotted ball of yarn,
Impossible to unravel.

The more I tug at a thread,
The tighter the knot pulls.
Unyielding, it tests me,
Questioning my intentions.
How can I release this pain,
This hurt that clings to me?

I pause, taking a deep breath,
And realize that perhaps the answer
Lies not in forceful unraveling,
But in gentle acceptance and patience.

With each passing moment, I learn
To sit with this discomfort,
To listen to its whispers,
And find the lessons hidden within.

Dreaming of You

Your smile
Those beautiful brown eyes
Always sparkling with a hint of mischief
Make me feel
like I'm the only one in your world

As thoughts of you dance in my mind
A contented smile graces my lips
I turn over, pulling the covers tight
Cocooning myself in warmth and comfort

In that moment
I'm reminded of your strong embrace
Holding me close, making me feel safe and secure
As if nothing could ever harm me

Reminding me that
With you by my side
I can face the world

Early Mornings

Listening to the quiet hum of the fridge
The slightest creaks of the house
The gentle snores of the children.

Sitting with a warm cup of tea
Watching the steam as it dances through the air.

Looking out of the window
Watching the trees sway in the breeze.

I open my door and step outside.
The birds are calling with their sweet song.

The start of a new day,
A chance to right the wrongs of yesterday
A day to make new memories,
And have new adventures.

Early mornings.

A time to reflect,
To pause
To breathe
To close my eyes and savour that first sip of tea.

Awakening

A sensation stirs deep within me
Gradually rising
Seeking expression
Wanting to be heard

An intense longing quickens my heart
Pressure mounting like steam craving release
'Set me free,' it whispers
'I am meant to feel
To take shape and form.'

It demands my attention
Refusing to be ignored
I close my eyes, inhale deeply
Surrendering to its power

In this moment
I embrace the surge
Ready to transform this raw energy
Into something tangible and real

Heartache

A dull ache nestles in the pit of my stomach,
Despair and hopelessness take hold
A heavy stillness descends
Dimming my world
Muting its vibrancy
Light fades as darkness envelops me
Joy and brightness become distant memories
I'm like a boat on a vast lake
Slowly drifting from the shore
The familiar blurs at the edges
Land and water merge into one
My heart, too, seems to dissolve
Melting into the fabric of my being
In this haze of melancholy
I float, untethered and alone

Sunrise

I blink once,
Then twice,
Unsure if my eyes are playing tricks on me.
I open them wide to absorb the beauty before me.
My thoughts settle,
Reflecting the stillness of the world around me.
My breath slows,
In sync with the ripples dancing across the water's
surface.
In the distance, a bird sings its morning melody,
As the sun rises in all its splendor just above the horizon.
I can almost hear it whisper,
"Good morning. It's going to be a beautiful day."

Taking up Space

What does it mean to take up space?
What is space?
Space is where you are in relation to those around you
The area that you occupy

Not just with your body
But with your voice
Your thoughts
Your opinions

Being who you are
Not questioning yourself
Doubting yourself

You matter
Your voice matters
As do your thoughts and opinions
So let yourself be heard

Don't be afraid
Be who you are meant to be
And take up SPACE

Whispers of the Heart

What is it that you truly want?
What does your soul desire?
Dig deep into your heart
And listen closely

Your heart holds no secrets
The truth waits patiently
Calling out with its steady beat
A gentle rhythm just for you

Quiet your mind
Still your thoughts
And let the noise fade away.

What you hear may surprise you
A truth waiting to be uncovered
Embrace this clarity
For it has always been within you

Ocean Waves

I watch the waves crash against the shore
Their powerful sounds fill my ears
I imagine my soul being cleansed
As negativity and sorrow wash away
Light begins to break through
Cracks forming in the walls I've built
Slowly and steadily
Like the waves that keep coming
With each crash upon the sand
I feel renewed and restored
In this moment
I am one with the ocean
Its waves carrying away my worries
Leaving only peace in their wake